MW01124260

GOD'S NEED AND GOD'S GOAL

Witness Lee

Living Stream Ministry
Anaheim, CA • www.lsm.org

First Edition, August 2011.

ISBN 978-0-7363-4813-3

Published by

Living Stream Ministry
2431 W. La Palma Ave., Anaheim, CA 92801 U.S.A.
P. O. Box 2121, Anaheim, CA 92814 U.S.A.

Printed in the United States of America

11   12   13   14   15   16   17   /   9   8   7   6   5   4   3   2   1

CONTENTS

PREFACE

This book contains seven messages that were originally published in serial form in *The Ministry of the Word* magazine from February through August of 1964. The last four messages were spoken during a New Year's conference in the church in Taipei in January 1957; the date and place of speaking for the first three messages are not known.

CHAPTER ONE

GOD'S NEED

Scripture Reading: Luke 14:16-17; 15:3-4, 8, 20-24; Matt. 22:1-3

Luke 14:17 says, "Come, for all things are now ready." This is a declaration of God in the universe: "Come, for all things are now ready." This is a precious utterance. The words *come* and *ready* refer to both God and us. God is ready, but we need to come. I hope that we all can recite this sentence: "Come, for all things are now ready."

MAN HAVING FEELINGS ONLY FOR HIS NEED

Today it is not my intention to preach the word or to study the Bible; I only desire to give a testimony. The Lord in His grace has led me in my living and work to see, understand, and live according to one matter. Therefore, I am happy and willing to testify concerning this matter, which the Lord has enabled me to see, obtain, enter into, and enjoy.

I want to speak of *God's need*. When I first began to work for God, I did not see God's need; I saw only man's need. It is easy to understand that man has needs, but do we have a sense of God's need? For example, preachers pay attention to man's need when they speak of the salvation that is available for sinners. Their speaking is based on the thought that human beings have failed and are in need of victory over sin, or that human beings are indifferent and in need of encouragement. In addition, they also speak of man's need for power, love, faithfulness, holiness, vigor, and so forth. Even when we receive light in reading the Word or in listening to messages, our light almost always relates to *man's need*.

Consequently, since our heart is focused on man's need, our eyes see only man's need. It is easy for us to see that people are cold and indifferent and that they are not filled with the Holy Spirit. It is also easy for us to see the need to preach the Word. It is not uncommon for a preacher to say, "The harvest is ripe, but the workers are few. There are so many people in need of salvation! These human souls are precious. I cannot bear to see them being cast into the lake of fire. Therefore, I need to preach." Everywhere I go, I meet people who say, "We are weak, and we have many failures. We need you to come and help us." This shows that our focus is on man's need.

GOD HAVING A NEED

Today by the Lord's grace we need to turn our eyes from the earth to heaven to see a need that is immensely greater than man's need—God's need. Without seeing God's need, it is difficult for people, who do not have a sense of need, to be saved. Furthermore, without seeing God's need, it is difficult for those who are saved to have a heavenly living or to obtain power and faith. May these words lead us to see the need on God's side so that our attention can be shifted from man to God.

God's Need Being Greater Than Man's Need

Some may ask, "Who has a greater need in the universe, man or God?" The Bible shows that God's need is primary, whereas man's need is secondary. Let us compare and see who has a greater need.

We know that sinners need salvation, but have we ever considered that salvation needs sinners? Yes, sinners need salvation, but salvation needs sinners. We often say that a certain person needs the power of the Holy Spirit, but conversely, we should ask, "Does not the power of the Holy Spirit need a person?" Likewise, many people think that a wandering son needs his father, but very few think that the father needs his wandering son to return.

In Luke 15 there is a story of the prodigal son whose garment was worn and who was hungry, thirsty, and filthy. In response to these needs, his father prepared the best robe, a ring, sandals, and a feast of a fattened calf. Still I would ask, "Whose need was greater—the son's or the father's?" The son was not happy without his father, but the father was not happy without his son. Those who know God would say that the father had a greater need. When the prodigal son returned home, there was a robe waiting for him. The son was not even expecting the robe. When the son returned, he said, "Father, I have sinned against heaven and before you; I am no longer worthy to be called your son" (v. 21). Without waiting for the son to finish his speaking, the father said to his slaves, "Bring out quickly the best robe and put it on him" (v. 22). The word *the* in verse 22 is precious because it shows that a robe was prepared by the father and was waiting for the son. While the father was preparing the robe, perhaps he said, "I have made a robe for my older son, but I have to make another robe, which will be the best robe, because my younger son is wandering outside and has not returned."

The father did not even have to tell the slaves where to find the robe. The father only said, "Bring out quickly the best robe." It seems as if the slaves knew where to find the robe because everyone knew that the father had prepared a robe, the best robe, for his son. This is the reason I say that it was the robe that was waiting for the son, not the son who was waiting for the robe. This speaks of the father's need, not the son's need. We should not see merely man's need; we need to see God's need even more. We all need to go and cry out to the world, "God needs man!"

ALL THINGS BEING NOW READY

In the Bible God likens His salvation to a dinner (14:16). Have you ever heard someone invite a guest, saying, "I would like to invite you to dinner because I am concerned that you have nothing to eat"? If someone invited me in this way, I probably would rather be hungry than eat dinner with him. We do not invite someone to dinner because he is in need of our dinner but because our dinner needs him. We invite people to dinner because we want them to come and enjoy our dinner, not because they are hungry.

It is not unusual for employees to refuse to work or for students to refuse to go to class, and it is not too strong to say that we often refuse God's invitation to dinner. This really grieves

His heart. If we were to see God's need, we would realize that it is quite easy to be saved. This is because God needs man even more than man needs Him. If we see this, we will say, "Thank the Lord, it was not me but God who was more concerned that I needed to be saved. It was not me but God who was more concerned that I needed power. It was not me but God who was more concerned that I needed faith. It was not me but God who was more concerned that I needed to be fervent."

We need to see that God truly needs us. Actually, there is no one who feels that he needs God, and there is no one who seeks God (Rom. 3:11). There is none. It is God who seeks man, and it is God who finds man. It is not we who want God; it is God who wants us. It is not we who choose God; it is God who chooses us. It is not we who love God; it is God who loves us. Our Lord was incarnated so that we could receive Him.

If we see that God needs us more than we need Him, we will realize that it is quite easy to be saved and to be faithful. We will even be able to say, "O God, it is not me who needs You; it is You who needs me. It is not that I need Your grace because I am weak but that Your grace needs my weakness." We should be able, like Paul, to say, "Most gladly therefore I will rather boast in my weaknesses that the power of Christ might tabernacle over me" (2 Cor. 12:9). The power of Christ cannot be manifested without our weaknesses. We should thank God that our weaknesses give Him the opportunity to shine forth. Although we certainly cannot do anything without God, He cannot be expressed to others without us. The more Paul boasted in his weaknesses, the more God shined forth from him. Paul even declared, "Where sin abounded, grace has superabounded" (Rom. 5:20). It is not light bulbs that need electricity; it is electricity that needs light bulbs to express its power as light.

If you think that your children are so troublesome, you need to realize that the more children you have, the more opportunity there is for you to be connected to God, just as a light bulb is connected to electricity. If you are afraid of being bothered by people, you need to realize that every troublesome person whom you encounter is another opportunity to be connected to God. God supplies us according to our need. This is a principle.

When we are weak, His strength can be displayed. When we fail, His victory can be displayed. When we are poor, His riches can be displayed.

"COME, FOR ALL THINGS ARE NOW READY"

We need to come, for all things are now ready. There is no need for us to bring anything or to exert any effort, because the Lord has prepared everything for us. We should not only come but also open ourselves to fully enjoy Him. If a person is not saved, he needs to come and receive salvation, and if a person is saved, he needs to come and enjoy salvation. Some are saved but are not overcoming; some are saved but are not filled with the Holy Spirit; some are saved but are not living a heavenly life; some are saved but are without peace. We need to come as we are, without struggling and striving, no matter what our condition is. If we lack power, if we lack faith, or if we lack a fervent pursuit, we need only to come because all things are now ready.

One day two foreign soldiers came to the meeting place in Tsingtao to buy wine. The brothers who were there told them that the meeting place had no wine for sale. The soldiers were surprised because a verse written on the outside wall said, "Come, for all things are now ready." They asked the brothers, "Does this not mean that people can come and buy wine to drink?" When they asked this, the brothers encouraged them to come and receive salvation. Like these soldiers, we need to come because all things are now ready. We need to come to the Lord with our sins and with our weaknesses so that we can meet His need to be expressed through us.

CHAPTER TWO

RESPONDING TO GOD'S NEED

Scripture Reading: Luke 14:16-17

In Luke 14:16-17 Jesus spoke to one of the rulers of the Pharisees, saying, "A certain man was making a great dinner and invited many; and he sent his slave at the dinner hour to say to those who had been invited, Come, for all things are now ready." Again, I hope that we all would be able to recite the last sentence: "Come, for all things are now ready." The two most crucial words in this sentence are *come* and *ready*. *Ready* is a precious word in the Bible. Do you want to be saved? Salvation is ready! Do you want to be victorious? Victory is ready! Do you want to be filled with the Holy Spirit? The filling of the Holy Spirit is ready! Everything on God's side is ready; God has accomplished and prepared everything. On man's side, however, there is still a need to come. Since God has prepared everything, man needs only to come and receive. God has prepared salvation for all the people in the world, but not everyone has been saved, because not everyone has come to God. The Holy Spirit has been poured out, but not everyone has received this outpouring, because not everyone has come to God.

Although all things are ready on the Lord's side, if a person is unwilling to come to God, he cannot be saved, victorious, or fervent. The burden of this chapter is more on our coming than on God making everything ready.

MAN'S NEED SHOWING GOD'S NEED

In the universe there are two aspects of need: man's need and God's need. In the parable in Luke 15, the son needs the robe, but the robe also needs the son. When these needs are considered in comparison, man's need is not as great as God's need. Matthew 22:2 says, "The kingdom of the heavens has become like a king who prepared a wedding feast for his son." Man surely needs to come to the feast, but God needs man to come to the feast.

Actually, our need shows that God has a need; our need reveals God's need. Just as a son needs joy, a father also needs joy. Any lack that we may feel speaks of a corresponding need of God. Our lack of joy, for example, reveals God's need to be our joy. Our need reveals God's need; our need shows the need of heaven, that is, the need of God.

People often say, "I need zeal. I need faithfulness. I need faith." This kind of speaking reveals that these needs correspond to God's need to be these things to us. When there is no rest in a heart on earth, there is also no rest in heaven. When there is no joy in a heart on earth, there is a need related to joy in heaven.

In John 4 there is a record of a man asking an immoral woman for a drink (v. 7). This man was the Son of God, our Lord Jesus. Although the Lord Jesus asked the woman for a drink, did He really want only some water to drink? Furthermore, did the woman even give Him water to drink? No. The Lord was thirsty because He met a woman whose heart was thirsty. When the woman heard the Lord speak to her about living water, she drank of this water from Him, and then she went into the city to testify of the Lord. She did not give the Lord a drink, but instead, she drank of the Lord's living water. When she was no longer thirsty, the Lord also was no longer thirsty. When the disciples returned and offered Him some food to eat, He did not eat, because He was neither hungry nor thirsty: "The disciples therefore said to one another, Has anyone brought Him anything to eat? Jesus said to them, My food is to do the will of Him who sent Me and to finish His work" (vv. 33-34). God's work is to satisfy man's need.

The parable of the prodigal son in Luke 15 also shows that when there is an unhappy son outside the house, there is an unhappy father inside the house. The extent of our need reveals the extent of God's need. We need God, but God needs us even more. God needs man more than man needs God. If we see this, we will thank and praise God.

GOD'S NEED BEING TO GIVE

God's need is not related to us giving Him something but to Him giving us Himself. He wants to give us Himself. God's need is not related to us doing something for Him but to Him doing something in us. God's need is not related to us giving Him something because He is poor. Rather, His need is related to Him being able to give us something because He is rich. God has everything, and He only wants us. God's only need is related to man and even is man. Everything was prepared in the father's house in Luke 15. The only thing that was missing was his wandering son. Likewise, when God gains us, He has no lack.

"Come, for all things are now ready." If someone who is invited to a feast brings a loaf of bread with him, the host will not be happy. When we go to a feast, we should not bring anything except an empty stomach. Whenever I am invited to a saint's home for a meal, I always come with an empty stomach, because I know that the host will encourage me to eat more. When I eat at home, I can eat less, but when I eat with the saints in their home, it is not polite to eat just a little. Every host enjoys seeing her guests eat all the food that she has prepared. Likewise, God wants us to come to His feast so that He can meet all our need.

"Come, for all things are now ready." God does not want us to give something to Him; neither does He want us to do something for Him. When we come, we should not come with our hands full of things, such as our own faith and zeal. We should put aside our faith and zeal. God is not focused on these things; He cares only that our heart would be empty so that He can impart Himself into us. From the beginning God has been desirous of giving Himself to man, not of man giving something to Him. We have nothing to give to Him, but He has something to give to us.

RESPONDING TO GOD'S NEED WITH CONSECRATION

How should we respond to God's need? The proper response is to consecrate ourselves to meet His need. Although some may say that *come* in this verse refers to faith, it also speaks of

consecration. God has a need, and we need to consecrate ourselves to respond to His need.

Many of us have an improper understanding of consecration. We think that consecration is a dreadful matter because
it will result only in the end of our enjoyment of the pleasures
of the world. However the universe contains more than just
the earth, and there is more than just man in the universe. The
universe contains both the heavens and the earth and both
God and man. We need to consecrate ourselves in order to enjoy
the heavenly things and God; consecration is not a matter of
dread but of joy.

Once I met a young lady in a meeting. Although she was
saved, she was quite fashionable in her attire and adornment.
After the meeting she came to me and asked, "Is it all right for
me to watch movies after I am saved?" I realized that it would
be difficult to give her an answer. If I said, "You should not
watch movies," she could be stumbled by my word to the point
that she would no longer desire to follow the Lord. However, if
I said, "It is okay to watch movies," it would confirm that her
love for the world was acceptable. Finally, I said to her, "If a little
child is playing with a knife, what is the best way to safely
take the knife from his hand?" She had a keen mind, and she
immediately said, "This is very simple. I would put some candy
and an apple on the floor. When the child sees the candy and the
apple rolling on the floor, he will drop the knife and pick them
up." I then asked, "How can you be certain that the child would
drop the knife?" She replied, "In order to pick up the candy and
the apple, which are better than the knife, he would have to drop
the knife. He would even lose interest in the knife." I responded,
saying, "Your answer is perfect. This is how God operates in us
to make us give up things like movies."

To consecrate ourselves means that we are dropping a "knife"
in order to pick up something much better. When we consecrate
ourselves to God, we can enjoy all God's riches. For example,
when we willingly consecrate ourselves to God, we touch God's
love, and when we give everything to God, we receive everything that we need from God.

In John 17:10 the Lord Jesus said, "All that is Mine is
Yours, and Yours Mine." Because the Lord Jesus was standing

on the position of consecration, He could say, "All that is Mine is Yours," and He also could say, "And Yours Mine." If we truly see the riches of our God, we would be able to say this word and even desire to say this word. If I were speaking to a wealthy man who was willing to give me everything that he had, why would I not be willing to say, "All that is mine is yours, and yours mine"? Our God is so rich! Why would we hesitate to say this to Him? What are we afraid of losing? As long as we give everything that we have to Him, He is willing to give us everything that He has. We should not hesitate in our consecration. Consecration is for us to obtain God and enjoy all His riches: "Come, for all things are now ready."

CHAPTER THREE

SATISFYING GOD'S NEED

Scripture Reading: Luke 14:17

God has a need in the universe. God does not need man to give Him something, because with Him there is no lack. God needs only a group of people who would consecrate themselves as empty vessels to receive His riches.

CONSECRATION BEING A GAIN, NOT A LOSS

Consecration is not a sacrifice or a loss but a gain and an enjoyment. Consecration does not mean that we agree to do something for God but that we agree to allow God to do something for us. Consecration means that we cease to work and instead allow God to work. Because we are filled with concepts related to the law, we think that we must do something for God, be zealous for God, or accumulate some merit before God. This thought does not come from God. This is the principle of the law, not the principle of grace. Everything that God gives to us is free. In the kingdom of God there are no commercial transactions; everything is freely given and freely received. However, in Satan's kingdom everything is a commercial transaction; that is, something must be given in order for something to be received. God does not deal with us in this way. If God did not provide us with sunlight, for example, there is nothing that we could give Him in order to receive sunlight. Without God not one blade of grass or one flower would grow, no matter how much money we could give Him.

It offends God when we try to conduct a "business transaction" with Him. How much money is one breath of air or one drop of water worth? Some may say, "It is easy to determine the value of water because every month I pay a small water fee, and I also buy water for drinking and laundering." It may seem as if we were buying water, but we are actually buying a service from the water company; the water itself has been freely given to us by God. If God did not provide us with water, there would be no amount of money that we could pay to a water company in order to obtain even a drop of water. Everything in creation has been freely given to us by God. Just as everything in creation is free, everything related to redemption is also free. Whatever has not been freely given to us by God is not grace. Consecration does not involve us giving something to God; it involves us stopping our work so that God can do His work. If we see this, it will be a great turning point in our experience.

<h3 style="text-align:center">CONSECRATED ONES
BEING FULL OF JOY AND AT REST</h3>

Many of us work in different places and on different jobs. Do we have a sense of joy when we are at work? Do we have a sense of rest? If we are a consecrated person, we will surely be full of joy and rest. A brother testified that when he consecrated himself to the Lord in prayer, he was so happy that he wanted to jump. The more he prayed, the happier he became. He said that he felt a sense of joy throughout his body. It even seemed to him as if his feet were happy and smiling. After consecration God gives us boundless joy.

Psalm 42:5 says, "Why are you cast down, O my soul? / And why are you disquieted within me? / Hope in God, for I will yet praise Him / For the salvation of His countenance." The psalmist exhorted his soul to hope in God, for he saw the salvation of God's countenance. Verse 11 continues, "Hope in God, for I will yet praise Him, / The salvation of my countenance and my God." Joy is a manifestation of God's salvation in our countenance. Do we express salvation in our countenance? Many people have a long face when they rise up in the morning, a face lacking in salvation. Such a face is not the face of a consecrated one.

One day a sister from a poor family was riding on a bus. As she thought about the Lord, she became so joyful that she could not sit still. The other passengers on the bus looked at her with curious eyes because they could not reconcile her obvious joy with her situation of poverty. The conductor even said sarcastically, "You look like you are going to receive an inheritance from a rich man who has died." Instead of getting angry, the sister said, "Yes! My Lord died for me, and He has given to me a heavenly inheritance." Because she knew the Lord, she expressed the Lord's salvation in her countenance everywhere she went.

If we do not express salvation in our countenance, it means that we are not standing in the position of consecration. If we do not have joy and happiness in our daily life, we have not yet been brought into the Lord to enjoy His riches. Consecration is a great turning point in a believer's life; it is also the turning point in our work. Every Christian should go through the gateway of consecration.

GOING THROUGH
THE GATEWAY OF CONSECRATION

How should we consecrate ourselves? It is very simple. We need to bring our position, our work, our family, and our all to God, handing them over completely to Him through prayer. When we go before the Lord in this way and yield ourselves to Him, the Lord will bear the responsibility, not us. This is consecration.

The Lord has led me through such an experience of consecration. One morning I felt strongly that I had to pray. While I was praying, the Lord showed me that I needed to go through the gateway of consecration. Kneeling before the Lord, I confessed my sins and then handed over my ability and my speaking to Him. I also offered my wife to Him, saying, "Lord, You have given my wife to me; I hand her over to You." I also offered my children, one by one, to Him, saying, "Lord, they are Your children; I hand them over to You. Furthermore, I hand over everything else that I have, including my furniture and my clothing to You." We should hand ourselves over to the Lord in a detailed way.

If we are willing to have such a consecration before the Lord, we will enjoy all that He has. We must hand over everything we have, both within and without, to Him.

STANDING IN THE POSITION OF CONSECRATION

After going through the gateway of consecration, we need to stand in the position of consecration by faith. Consecration does not mean that the circumstances of our living will change. For example, our children and our spouses may still trouble us. In such situations, however, we need to stand in the position of consecration by faith. The devil seeks to frustrate man's salvation in two ways. First, he hinders man from being saved, and second, he causes believers to be skeptical and full of doubt. Before a person is saved, the devil tries to prevent him from being saved, but after a person is saved, the devil tries to make him doubt his salvation. Likewise, before a believer consecrates himself, the devil tries to hinder him from consecrating himself to the Lord, but after a believer consecrates himself, the devil tries to make him doubt his consecration. This is the devil's cunning scheme.

When a brother, who was a farmer, went to work in his field, he was reminded of his need to consecrate himself to the Lord. Therefore, he prayed, saying, "Lord, I consecrate everything to You." Shortly thereafter, a question from the devil entered his mind, asking, "Have you truly consecrated yourself?" The farmer began to have some doubts, and he said to himself, "Just in case, I will consecrate myself again." So he prayed, "Lord, I give everything to You. I give You my house, my field, and everything I have." After he worked for a period of time, the same question again came to him: "Have you really consecrated yourself?" When he began to have some doubt, he realized the scheme of the devil. In response, he inserted a wooden stake into his field so that he would be able to point to the place of his consecration. He said to himself, "If the devil comes again, I will show him the evidence of my consecration." After a short while, the devil again asked, "Have you truly consecrated yourself?" The farmer quickly responded, "Go away! I have consecrated myself to the Lord, and this stake is the place of my consecration."

When we offer ourselves to God, He is pleased to accept us. We have no cause for doubt. When we place ourselves on the altar, our offering of ourselves is counted by God. We should have no uncertainty about our consecration or about the Lord's acceptance of our consecration. There was once a brother who had nothing to give to the Lord. He was in poor health, and his situation showed no signs of improvement. When many of the brothers began to consecrate themselves to the Lord and were full of rejoicing, he was concerned that he had nothing to offer to the Lord. The only thing he could think of to offer to the Lord was his wife, who loved the Lord very much. Even though he was afraid that the Lord would call her for His work, he still offered her to the Lord, saying, "Lord, I have nothing to give you, but I offer my wife to You." In his mind this consecration was merely a polite gesture to the Lord; he fully expected that the Lord would not accept his offering. Little did he know that the Lord truly wanted his wife to work for Him. When the brother learned of this, he was very disappointed. He later testified, saying, "I was merely trying to be polite to the Lord when I consecrated my wife to Him. Little did I know that He would not be polite in return."

Once we consecrate ourselves, we are in the position of consecration. We must see that this position is crucial. Once we stand in such a position, we should not be afraid of anything. The devil is afraid of our consecration, and he is happy as long as we do not stand in the position of consecration. We need to say to the Lord, "You are the Lord; You should gain everything that I have." This word will not only touch God's heart but also scare the devil away.

A sister who was serving as a missionary was traveling on a boat that encountered some pirates on the sea. She prayed and received a word: "I belong to Jesus." When the pirates came to her, she courageously said, "I belong to Jesus. You cannot harm me unless Jesus wants you to harm me." This word scared them, and they were fearful of harming her. One of the pirates, however, noticed that she was wearing a watch, and he demanded that she give him the watch. She spoke to the pirate in a loud voice, saying, "I cannot give my watch to you. I cannot give my watch to a pirate. If you want it, you will have to use force to take it because I will not give it to you." The pirate then forcefully took the watch. When the leader of the pirates heard about this incident, he returned the watch to her. At this point she spoke to the leader, saying, "Look at the dirty deck. Are you not concerned about sickness? You should clean the deck." Because of her speaking, the pirates cleaned the deck. She did not suffer any harm, and she was able to grasp the opportunity to preach the gospel to them.

To stand in the place of consecration means to let the Lord be the Lord, allowing Him to control everything. After consecrating your child to the Lord, you should ask the child, "Whose child are you?" Surely he will say, "You are my father, and I am your child." Then you have to say, "Formerly, you belonged to me, but you are no longer mine." The child might say, "If I no longer belong to you, I still belong to my mother." you have to tell him, "You no longer belong to your mother either. We have consecrated you to the Lord; now you belong to Him." Then when your child makes a mistake, you will have the ground to show him the Lord's interest in the matter, which will give the Lord the opportunity to work in your child's situation. Many people rise up in the morning and pray to the Lord, saying, "Today I consecrate everything to You." But when their children make a mistake, they quickly act as if their children belong to them, saying, "We are your parents. We told you not to do bad things. Since you did not listen to us, we are going to punish you." Parents who act in this way chase the Lord away and give Him no opportunity to be the Lord.

CONSECRATED ONES HAVING AUTHORITY

We receive authority as soon as we pass through the gateway of consecration. In Exodus 32 God burned with anger against the children of Israel after they worshipped the golden calf. He wanted to consume them, and He said to Moses, "Your people, whom you brought up out of the land of Egypt, have corrupted themselves" (v. 7). However, Moses responded, saying, "Why does Your anger burn against Your people, whom You brought out of the land of Egypt with great power and with a mighty hand?" (v. 11). With his word Moses confirmed that this matter was God's responsibility. Because Moses was an absolutely consecrated person, he properly turned over all responsibility related to this situation to God.

Few among us can say, "My prayers are for the Lord, not

for myself." Once there was a brother who had a long-standing health problem related to his stomach, and he often prayed earnestly about his illness. One day I asked him, "When you pray for your illness, is it for yourself or for the Lord?" Saints, have you consecrated yourselves? Are you for the Lord? Someone may say, "I have entrusted everything to the Lord." But merely entrusting things to the Lord is not enough; you need to hand them over to Him. To say that you have entrusted yourself to the Lord is like depositing money in the bank for safekeeping but which you can still withdraw at any time. You may have entrusted everything to the Lord, but the authority to use the things remains in your hands. You should turn all authority over to the Lord; only in this way can the Lord truly bear our responsibilities.

A sister who was working for the Lord in a certain locality lived by faith. One day she received a letter informing her that two classmates would be coming to visit on a certain day. She had no food, and she became quite anxious. She thought, "When my classmates come to visit and I have nothing to offer, they will say that my God is false. I cannot allow my guests to go away hungry." She then prayed earnestly for this matter, and her faith was strengthened. She said, "Lord, if You are not concerned about being shamed, neither am I. You are the One who takes care of my living. If my classmates come to see me, and I have nothing for them, this is not my concern; it is Your concern." At that very moment, a brother came to visit her and gave her a small box that another person had entrusted to him for her. She opened the box and saw that there were bread, eggs, and other food items. The Lord truly bore her responsibility.

When the Lord and His disciples were in a boat crossing the sea, a great tempest arose. The disciples were afraid and anxious, so they woke up the Lord who was sleeping in the boat, saying, "Lord, save us; we are perishing!" (Matt. 8:25). Their anxiety showed that they were not standing in the position of consecration. If they were standing in the position of consecration, they might have said to the wind and waves, "Waves, beat higher! Wind, blow stronger! The Lord is here. Since He is sleeping at the rear of the boat, we will sleep in the front." We have no need to fear anything when we are standing in the position of consecration.

We need to see that Jesus is Lord. We should have no fear; we need only to hand ourselves over to Him because He is Lord. We need to rejoice and be at peace daily by standing in the place of consecration. We should yield everything that we have to Him and let Him do everything for us. This will not put Him to shame; it will glorify Him. He desires mercy and not sacrifice (9:13). Mercy is what He gives to us, whereas sacrifice is what we give to Him. The Lord does not want us to give Him anything; His only desire is that we enjoy what He gives us. In Luke 14 the Lord spoke of a certain man who was making a great dinner and who sent his slave at the dinner hour to invite some to eat, saying, "Come, for all things are now ready" (v. 17). We should simply come. When we come, we will enter into His riches.

CHAPTER FOUR

THE SPIRITUAL SIGNIFICANCE
OF THE NEW YEAR

Scripture Reading: Gen. 1:14, 16; Jer. 8:7, 20; Mal. 4:2; Col. 2:16-17; Rev. 21:5, 23; 22:2; Ezra 7:9; 8:21, 23

THE VISIBLE BODY SPEAKING FORTH
THE INVISIBLE CONTENT

Although all the countries in the world use the Gregorian calendar, that is, the so-called solar calendar, those who study calendars acknowledge that the Chinese lunar calendar is more compatible with the seasons of the year. For example, spring begins during the first month of the lunar calendar; it can be said that the beginning of the lunar calendar marks the beginning of a year. This beginning, like all the visible and physical things created by God in the universe, has spiritual significance. Behind everything that is visible and physical, there is something that is invisible and spiritual. For example, every person has a body, but the purpose of our body is to contain the human life. The body is tangible and visible, but the life within the body is intangible and invisible. Although there are both visible and invisible aspects of man, the reality of a man is determined by what is invisible. When a person dies, his spirit and soul depart, but his visible body remains. Nevertheless, everyone knows that a person is no longer with us when he dies, even though his body remains. The reality of a man does not depend on what is visible and tangible but on what is invisible and intangible.

Similarly, all the systems in the universe have outward forms and inward contents; the forms are visible, whereas the contents are invisible. The outward, visible forms speak of the inward, invisible contents. In the universe some of the systems include the sun and the moon, and other systems relate to time. There are three hundred and sixty-five days in a year, thirty days in a month, and twenty-four hours in a day. Many people know that these systems of time are related to astronomy, and they even speak of how the times and seasons affect living things in creation. However, if we ask the ones who knew these things to speak of how the inward and invisible matters relate to these systems, they will be perplexed because they can see only the outward forms. They cannot comprehend the operation of the inward contents.

By studying the Word of God, in the first chapter of Genesis we can see that God created light-bearers, including the sun and the moon, for signs, for seasons, and for days and years (v. 14). At the end of the Bible, Revelation 21:23 says, "The city has no need of the sun or of the moon that they should shine in it, for the glory of God illumined it, and its lamp is the Lamb." Neither the sun nor the moon will be needed in the New Jerusalem, because God will be the light, and the Lamb will be the lamp. Hence, there will be no need for the shining of the sun or of the moon. This indicates that days, months, and years, as well as seasons, are depictions of things that pertain to God. The sun and the moon are mere symbols, outward forms, but the inner reality is Christ. Even before we come to the end of the Bible, there is a word of promise concerning Christ at the end of the Old Testament, which says, "Unto you...will the Sun of righteousness arise" (Mal. 4:2). Since there is a sun in the heavens, we need to ask why there would be a need for the appearing of another sun. Those who know God will be able to answer that the sun in the heavens is an outward form that serves as a symbol of the invisible Sun, which is Christ. Christ is the light of the people in the world (John 1:4). People can truly touch light only when they touch Christ. Therefore, days, months, years, and seasons are symbols that have a mysterious content, which is Christ Himself.

DAYS, MONTHS, AND YEARS
BEING OPPORTUNITIES PREPARED BY GOD

Why did God order the universe according to days, months,

and years? Scientists tell us that the existence and growth of living things, whether plants or animals, are regulated by the cycles of days, months, and years. God has ordained days, months, and years for the existence and growth of living things. Anyone who has ever lived in northern China is aware of the fact that the time for planting and sowing is in the spring of every year. If the planting and sowing of seed are not accomplished during the spring, a farmer will say, "Let us wait until next year to plant our seed." If the time span of the universe consisted of one long day, there would be only one opportunity for life to exist and grow. Thus, if there were existence and growth during this period of time, there would be existence and growth, but if there were a failure to exist and grow, there would not be another opportunity for life to exist and grow. Thankfully, God has prepared and ordained numerous opportunities in the universe, not just one opportunity. If we experience a failure during one year, there will be another year. If our work is not successful this year, we can start again next year.

This is true not only in matters related to living things; it is true even in matters related to business, education, and a career. If we have not done well in our business this year, we can start again in the coming year. If we fail an exam this year, we do not have to be discouraged, because we can study more and take another exam next year. If we experience some failure in our career this year, we should not worry, because a new year is coming. We would not have much hope if the time frame of the universe consisted of one long year. Then those who failed in business or failed a college exam would not have another chance. Thankfully, this is not our situation, because there is always an opportunity next year, and if we are not discouraged, we can take advantage of the coming opportunity. The opportunity for a new beginning is related to God's good pleasure.

In God's arrangement we have opportunities not only from one year to the next but also from one month to the next. Merchants must make both yearly and monthly statements. They reconcile their accounts at the end of each year and at the end of each month. If business has not been good, there is always the hope that next year it will be better. Furthermore, God gives us opportunities not only year after year and month after month but also day after day. It is truly wonderful that we have a new opportunity every twenty-four hours. If we do not do well today, we can start again tomorrow. If we fail today, we can rest for a night and have a new opportunity in the morning. Days, months, and years are truly meaningful. Most living things grow day by day, month by month, and year by year. Human beings are no exception to this rule.

All these outward matters speak of spiritual matters. God is our sun and our light-bearer. We depend on Him for our existence and for our growth in life. He is constantly presenting us with opportunities to grow. Being defeated in a certain matter does not mean that we will have no further opportunities to overcome. According to the changing of days, months, and years, God gives us new opportunities every day, every month, and every year.

EVERY DAY, MONTH, AND YEAR BEING A NEW BEGINNING

In our spiritual life we have spiritual days, months, and years. In the Old Testament God charged the children of Israel to keep the passover before leaving Egypt. This was a great beginning. He wanted them to consider the month of Abib, the first month, to be the beginning of months, the first of the months of the year (Exo. 12:1-2; 34:18). The Israelites kept the passover as a new beginning; it was not a small beginning but a great beginning. Because of this beginning, they were able to serve God according to an order of worship in the tabernacle. The book of Numbers also speaks of "the beginnings of your months," which refers to times set according to new moons (10:10; 28:11). A new moon is a lesser beginning. The beginning of a year is a great beginning, whereas the beginning of a month is a lesser beginning. God also required the Israelites to worship daily in the morning and at night (Lev. 6:9, 12). The beginning of a day is a small beginning. The days, months, and years of the Israelites were full of spiritual significance. When we are saved, we experience the reality of the passover, which is a great and new beginning. Thereafter, God desires that we have a new beginning every month and even a new beginning every day.

When I was saved by the Lord's grace, I truly experienced the Feast of the Passover. At that time I had an earnest desire to pursue the Lord, read the Word, preach the gospel, and offer material things. However, as men, we are weak, and even though I had such a desire, I was not successful in practice. Instead, I failed frequently. As I look back at my life during those years, I feel as though I was short in reading the Word, poor in prayer, loose in preaching the gospel, and unfaithful in material offerings. Many times it seemed as if I had reached the end of a month marked by a waning and even a disappearing moon. Yet, amazingly, at these very moments a new spiritual moon would arrive. I was able to let the previous experiences pass and begin again as if it were the first day of a new month. From the first day of this new moon, my reading of the Word was fresh, my prayer was enjoyable, and my zeal for preaching the gospel was stirred up again. I was in the enjoyment of the shining of a new spiritual moon. This shining would last for several weeks, as if my experience, like the moon, were rising to the full. However, a full moon does not last very long; it was not uncommon to lose this sense of fullness in my spiritual pursuit. Consequently, at a certain point and often for no apparent reason, I would not feel like getting out of bed. I also would lose my desire to read the Bible, my strength for prayer, and my interest in preaching the gospel. This was the waning of my spiritual moon. After eight or ten days in this condition, it would seem as if the moon had disappeared completely. Rather than light, I had a sense only of darkness. Even in the midst of this discouragement, however, there would be the coming of a new moon. Then, once again, I would feel like getting up in the morning, reading the Bible, praying, and preaching the gospel. I believe that we all have had such experiences related to a spiritual new moon.

In addition to the experience of a new month, we also have experiences of a new day. For example, we may hear a message on the Lord's Day encouraging us to rise up early in the morning to draw near to the Lord, to read His Word, and to fellowship with Him. After hearing such a message, we may be touched throughout the day and look forward to the coming of the next morning. Consequently, we will rise up early the next day in order to have morning watch and to draw near to the Lord. As a result of this morning watch, we enjoy an overcoming life the whole day without a failure. With such an encouraging experience, we again rise up early the next morning to have fresh prayer and sweet fellowship with the Lord. Even though we may experience no failure in the morning, a little carelessness may cause us to lose our temper in a small way in the afternoon. Because of this little failure, we will be somewhat depressed and discouraged when we return home. Nevertheless, after resting at night we can have a new beginning when we rise up in the morning. We can pray to the Lord and fellowship with Him so that the brightness of His shining may rise up in us once again. This is the experience of a new day.

In spiritual matters we all experience new days, new months, and new years. The beginning of the approaching lunar year should not point us only toward a new day or a new month but to the beginning of a new spiritual year. We should have more than a new day or a new month; we should also have the experience of a new year. Regrettably, many Christians celebrate a new calendar year every year, but they never enter into a new spiritual year. Many Christians have been saved five, ten, or even twenty years, and at the end of a year they buy food and new clothes, put their houses in order, and close their business in preparation for the new year. While they celebrate the new year, they do not prepare themselves for a new year spiritually. Thus, there is no proper ending, no new preparation, and hence, no new beginning.

KEEPING A SPIRITUAL NEW YEAR
BEFORE GOD

At the end of the year, some saints not only enter into a new calendar year but also into a new spiritual beginning. At the end of the year and at the beginning of a new year, they go before God to review and settle their condition before God from the passing year. Just as a businessman settles his account at the end of the year, we should review our spiritual account before God. If we balance only our outward account but not our inward account, we will enter into a new calendar year but not into a new spiritual year.

I hope that from this year forward every saint will have a proper spiritual conclusion to a passing year and a proper beginning of a new spiritual year. Not only should we have a conclusion related to outward matters, such as our career, our education, and our domestic affairs, but even more, we should have a conclusion in regard to spiritual matters. At the end of a year, we need to go before God and settle the accounts related to our spiritual condition. We need to consider before the Lord how we have spent our time and the things in which we failed and in which we overcame. We need to consider the areas in which we responded to the Lord's demands and in which we rejected the Lord's will. We need to bring our spiritual condition before the Lord in order to settle accounts and have a proper clearance so that we can have a new beginning.

THE CHANGING OF DAYS, MONTHS, AND YEARS
DEPENDING ON LIGHT-BEARERS

There are two very important principles concerning days, months, and years. The first principle involves their relationship to light-bearers, and the second principle involves their relationship to death and resurrection. In regard to the first principle, days, months, and years are related to light-bearers, that is, to the sun and the moon. A day consists of the time that it takes for the earth to revolve on its own axis, whereas a year consists of the time that it takes for the earth to revolve around the sun. Every twenty-four hours the earth revolves on its axis, and during this time there is one appearing of the sun. Furthermore, every three hundred sixty-five days the earth revolves around the sun in the solar system. A day involves a small revolution, but a year involves a great revolution. Both the changing of a day and the changing of a year are in relation to the sun. The changing of a month is related to the revolution of the moon around the earth. Both the sun and the moon are light-bearers. Every changing of days, months, and years is related to light-bearers. Because there are light-bearers, there are days, months, and years.

Every change in our spiritual experience involves light,

whether it is a great change like a new year, a lesser change like a month, or a small change like a day. Whenever we encounter light, there is a change. When we met God, who is light (1 John 1:5), there was a change. When we met Christ, who is God and who is light (John 8:12; 9:5; 12:46), there was a change. God in Christ is our light-bearer. Without the sun, there are no days or years, and without the moon, there are no months. Likewise, if a person does not encounter God in Christ, there will be no spiritual change, either great or small. Every change in our spiritual condition depends upon meeting God.

In order to have a new spiritual year, we need to specifically seek God's face and meet Him. We should bring our condition, past and present, to Him and place it before Him in the light of His face in order to receive His shining. He is facing us, waiting for us, and open to us. We should not think that we are the ones who are seeking God; actually, He is seeking us and waiting for us. Rather than being closed, we should open ourselves to Him. We should not treat our days in a loose manner. When we approach a new calendar year, we should come to God and open ourselves to His light concerning not only the state of our earthly affairs but also the condition of our spiritual life. We need to spend some time in the presence of God, presenting our past and present condition to Him and allowing Him to shine on us. As the Spirit, He will come to us, and with His Spirit there will be light shining on the items that we place before Him. When we encounter God in Christ as the Spirit coming to us as light, we will have a new beginning. When we encounter light, we will also encounter God as the light-bearer. These encounters bring in changes that are like the changes associated with days, months, and years. If we want to have changes, from small changes to great changes, we must meet God.

THE PRINCIPLE OF DAYS, MONTHS, AND YEARS BEING DEATH AND RESURRECTION

I know of some brothers and sisters who have always fasted and prayed through the night at the end of a year, especially on New Year's Eve. They go before God, bringing their life and work and their spiritual condition from the previous year to

Him, praying about item after item in order to receive God's enlightenment. When they encounter His shining concerning their shortages, failures, weaknesses, and mistakes, they confess them before God and receive His forgiveness and cleansing. With the exposure of their defects and deficiency, they also pray to be supplied and filled with God. Through this, they receive fresh grace, fresh enlightenment, fresh power, and fresh promises from God. Thus, they have a new beginning before God. Their past is terminated, and there is a new beginning for their future. This illustrates the second principle related to days, months, and years, which is the principle of death and resurrection. The ending of a day and the beginning of a new day illustrate death and resurrection. Likewise, the ending of a month and a year and the beginning of a new month and a new year illustrate death and resurrection. The ending and the beginning of days, months, and years signify death and resurrection.

The course of our spiritual journey involves a continuing experience of death and resurrection. An ending and a beginning always are followed by another ending and another beginning. These endings and beginnings correspond to Paul's word in Philippians 3:13, which says, "Forgetting the things which are behind and stretching forward to the things which are before." *Forgetting the things which are behind* refers to an ending, and *stretching forward to the things which are before* refers to a new beginning.

On the first day of a new year we should realize that the previous year is behind us and that a new year, a new beginning, is before us. The former things have passed away, and all things should be new. In the light of the Lord, our former weaknesses, failures, and mistakes will come to an end, and we need not bring them with us. With a new year, we can have a new beginning, a good beginning, starting in resurrection. The meaning of the changing of days, months, and years is related to encountering God as light and to experiencing death and resurrection. We need to meet God, and we need an ending and a new beginning. We should not remain in our old experiences, whether good or bad, because both the good and the bad have been terminated so that we can begin anew.

THE CHANGING OF DAYS, MONTHS, AND YEARS
DEPENDING ON GOD HIMSELF

Every change within us, whether it is associated with days, months, or years, depends on God. God is light, and even death and resurrection are of God. Whenever we meet God, we meet light; when we meet God, we touch both death and resurrection. Whenever we meet God, we are in the presence of light; when we meet God, we enter into death and resurrection so that there is an ending and a new beginning.

God's work in the universe is a work of renewing. He wants to end the old things and begin something new. When His work is accomplished, He will be able to declare that all things are truly new (2 Cor. 5:17). The proper celebration of a new year is to have a new beginning. We need to go before God and touch His presence. When we touch God and meet God, we will enter into a new year and have a new beginning.

SEPARATED FROM THE PEOPLE IN THE WORLD

Meeting God in this way is not the same as the New Year celebrations of worldly people. People in the world celebrate the arrival of a new year outwardly, but they do not experience a new spiritual beginning. Their noisy way of celebration can be likened to the celebration of the children of Israel at the foot of Mount Sinai, who were sitting down to eat and drink and rising up to play. Their sitting down to eat and drink and rising up to play were related to idolatry (Exo. 32:4-6; 1 Cor. 10:7). Worldly people today celebrate the new year by sitting down to eat and drink and by rising up to play. When those who belong to God spend time to meet God at the beginning of a new year, their meeting with God is not a time for celebration. Rather, it is a time of sorrow, weeping, and fasting. When we see the desolation of our personal situation, the failures related to the church's condition, the need for salvation in many sinners, the shortage in function of many saints, the lack of accomplishment related to the Lord's will, and the frustration of God's plan, we will be full of sorrow and repentance.

Ezra 7:9 speaks of the first day of the first month, saying, "On the first day of the first month he began to go up from Babylon." Ezra left Babylon, a place of degradation, on the first day of the first month; this is very meaningful. According to 8:21, Ezra proclaimed a fast for all the Israelites who intended to return to the Holy Land so "that we might humble ourselves before our God to seek from Him a straight way for ourselves and for our little ones and for all our possessions." All the Israelites who left Babylon, a place of degradation and captivity, needed to fast on the first day of the first month to grieve, confess, regret, and repent before God, asking Him for His grace and mercy.

If, by God's mercy, we meet God and are enlightened by Him at the beginning of a new calendar year, we will mourn and weep instead of celebrate. We will fast instead of feasting and grieve instead of rejoicing. We will weep and grieve, and we will pray and petition. Then we truly will have a new beginning of a new spiritual year. May the Lord be merciful and gracious to us to bring us into a new spiritual year, year after year. May we go before Him and ask Him to give us a new beginning. May we be under His enlightenment and receive His mercy. Such a seeking will bring us into victory and deliver us from the worldliness and celebrations associated with a new calendar year.

CHAPTER FIVE

NOT BEING DISCOURAGED WHEN WE FALL

Scripture Reading: Isa. 55:8-9; 1 Sam. 2:6-7

THE SPIRITUAL PATH HAVING UPS AND DOWNS

In the preceding chapter we saw that the visible systems in the universe have spiritual significance. Now we need to see that these systems in the universe do not operate along a straight path. For example, there are mornings, and there are evenings; there are days, and there are nights; there are sunny days, and there are cloudy days; there are summers, and there are winters; and there are births, and there are deaths. Moreover, there are things that bring joy and things that bring sorrow; there are things that are beautiful and things that are ugly; and there are things that are sweet and fragrant and things that are rotten and stinking. In the entire universe it is hard to find any matter or principle that operates on a straight path. There are ups and downs associated with nearly everything. This is also true in regard to spiritual matters.

In our human considerations related to our spiritual life, nearly every Christian has the concept that the path of our spiritual life should be straight. After we are saved, it is our hope and desire to follow the Lord continuously for our whole life. However, this often does not happen. When we are revived, we again hope and desire to stand firm and to courageously follow a straight path without any further failure. In truth, no one's experience of walking reflects a straight path. Even though we are saved, we will fall inexplicably and involuntarily, and after we are revived, we later will fall again. At such times, we may wonder how we became so indifferent to the point of backsliding, and we may regard our situation as being so pitiful that it is impossible to rise up. Nevertheless, at a certain point and often just as inexplicably, we rise up and begin to love and pursue the Lord once again.

These experiences lead us to an important discovery about ourselves, the discovery that we are not dependable or consistent. When we hope and desire to stand, we fall without any seemingly logical explanation. When we think that we are finished, we likewise rise up again without any seemingly logical explanation. After we rise up, we often are even more determined to be careful and to remain on a straight path. However, at any time we can inexplicably fall again, because even though a will to stand is present with us, working it out is not (Rom. 7:18). In our mind and will there is a desire to walk along a straight path, but in our actual experience there are both falling and rising. We want the sky above us to always be bright without any sense of darkness, but there are always an evening and a night, and the sky always becomes dark at night. However, after the night there is the brightness of the coming day. Similarly, we rise and fall, fall and rise.

Can anyone say that he has had only an experience of rising from the time that he was saved and that his days have always been bright with no hint of darkness? I do not believe that such a brother or sister exists. Although our thoughts are focused on a straight line, God's thoughts are higher than our thoughts (Isa. 55:8-9), and He has ordained a path that is full of ups and downs (1 Sam. 2:6-7). After we experience a day, we will experience a night. After a summer there will be a winter, after a spring there will be an autumn, and after life there will be death. However, after death there will be resurrection. God's leading is not according to a straight line; it is a path with both ups and downs.

OUR CIRCUMSTANCES NOT ALWAYS BEING SMOOTH
OR ACCORDING TO OUR WISHES

When a brother who loves the Lord considers the matter of marriage, he thinks, "I am a young brother, I have received grace, and I really love the Lord. I have prayed and consecrated myself to the Lord, asking Him to prepare a good wife for me." A young sister who loves the Lord also will ask the Lord to prepare a good husband for her. When brothers or sisters ask the Lord for a good wife or a good husband, they mean a sister or a brother who loves the Lord as much as they do. Many young brothers and sisters pray in this way, but their prayers often seem to produce an opposite result. For nearly thirty years I have been observing God's children, and we have tried our best to help the brothers and sisters concerning their marriage, yet regardless of how much we try to help, the results never seem to match our ideal expectations.

Sometimes we had a feeling that it would be good if a certain seeking brother could marry a sister who truly loved the Lord. Or we thought that a brother who had much light and a sister who was quite spiritual would be a perfect couple. We felt good about both, and when we introduced them to each other, they too were pleased. After they were married, however, we discovered that the sister did not really love the Lord that much. Sometimes we felt that a good sister, who was even like Mary, should be introduced to the best brother, to one who loved the Lord very much. Little did we realize that the brother would turn out to be very fleshly after they were married.

We went to Tientsin to begin the work and establish the church in 1936. While we were there, we met a young brother who was in college and who really loved the Lord. Because we were at the initial stage of the church life, we considered him to be a treasure. At the same time, we knew a sister who loved the Lord very much and who also attended the same college. Eventually, they became acquainted with each other. One day the young brother came to fellowship with me and said, "Brother Lee, I have asked the Lord to give me a sister who loves Him. Do you think that this sister is suitable?" I said, "She is a good sister. If she is willing, it would be a wonderful match prepared by the Lord." When they were married, I was present at their wedding, and I even spoke a word. We were all very happy that this brother had been blessed to have such a precious sister. We believed that they were a good match for each other—one was spiritual and the other loved the Lord. As a couple, we also felt that they could serve the Lord. Regrettably, not long after they were married, the brother found out that the sister loved the world a great deal.

Even though some couples are very spiritual, and both the husband and wife love the Lord, their circumstances do not always turn out to be so ideal. Shortly after a couple was married, they began to have children. They prayed and asked the Lord to cause their children to love Him, to give themselves to Him, and to serve Him. However, even though the husband and wife both loved the Lord, their children did not love the Lord as much. The couple prayed continually, saying, "Lord, we give our children to You, and we pray that You would call them one by one." However, none of their children were called. There was another couple who wanted their children to be saved and attend the meetings, to listen to messages, and to conduct themselves properly. However, they did not want their children to be called to serve the Lord. Nevertheless, their first child was called, and so was their second. We were happy that the children were called, but the parents were not happy that they were called. Some saints want their children to be called, but God does not call them. Others are anxious over the thought of their children being called, but God intentionally seems to call them. This is very mysterious. Hearing this, some may wonder if it is possible for the parents and the children in a family to all love the Lord. While we have certainly seen situations involving a whole family loving the Lord, even then not every situation is according to our ideal. For example, the most spiritual son may meet an untimely death, but a less spiritual son lives a long life.

UPS AND DOWNS AND ADVERSITIES
CAUSING PEOPLE TO GROW IN LIFE

It is difficult for some to understand these situations. When a brother who loves the Lord marries a sister who loves the Lord, there can still be problems, and when a spiritual sister marries a spiritual brother, there also can be problems. Sometimes there is no problem with the brother and the sister, but their children grow up loving the world more than the Lord. Even when children love the Lord just as their parents do, this positive situation may not last long, because accidents and even death can occur. We have seen many situations like this in the past twenty to thirty years, and it was difficult for us to understand and comprehend the Lord's way.

However, now we can stand before the Lord and say that God's thoughts are not our thoughts and that His ways are higher than our ways (Isa. 55:8-9). We should remember that God has arranged systems in the universe that do not follow a straight line; rather, these systems involve ups and downs. Autumn follows spring, and winter follows summer. Night follows day, sorrow follows joy, and death follows life. A straight line is not God's way.

God's way is related to our growth in life. A wife who loves the Lord will have fewer opportunities to grow in life with a husband who loves the Lord than she will with a husband who does not love the Lord as much. Children who are disobedient cause their parents to grow in life more than children who love the Lord. If there is birth but no death, there will be little growth, and if there is day but no night, there also will be little growth.

Many animals and plants need overcast and rainy days as well as sunny days; they need night as well as day; they need winter as well as summer. I have lived in Southeast Asia for extended periods of time, and it is accurate to say that the food produced in a hot climate is not as tasty as our food. Their chickens and ducks and even their eggs are not as tasty as ours, and their fish are not of equal quality to ours because they have a summer climate all year. There are no cold days. Every day is a hot day, and the constant heat makes people miserable. Living things cannot flourish without cold weather. With hot and cold days and even daytime as well as nighttime temperatures, every living thing grows better. Even among the human race, people with smart minds and strong character are associated more with places that have variable seasons. This is God's arrangement.

FALLING ALSO BEING ACCORDING TO GOD'S WILL

If human life involved only birth but no death, only joy without sorrow, people would not experience much growth. A person who can stand without ever falling will not have much depth. Those who are deep in the Lord are the ones who have fallen the most. Hearing this, some may say, "Is this not the doctrine of doing evil that good may come, as in Romans 3:8?

Are you encouraging us to fall?" Although I wish that we all would fall so that we could grow, I am not saying that we should do evil that good may come. I often tell people that falling is not an easy matter. In fact, it is even more difficult to fall than it is to stand.

However, when God allows us to fall, we will have no way to escape; we will fall. David was very pious and spiritual in his living before the Lord. When we read the psalms that he wrote, we can see that he was a person who lived in the Lord's presence. However, he did not know himself, and one day the Lord seemingly said, "Do you think that you are pious? Do you think that you are spiritual? You need to see your real condition." As soon as God withdrew His hand, David fell; he had Uriah killed and took his wife, committing a great sin (2 Sam. 11:14-27; 12:9). When David was about to sin, God could have moved His finger just slightly, and David would have been preserved from committing these sins. However, instead of preserving David, God allowed him to fall and go through a dark night.

We should not have the thought that it is difficult for a Christian to stand. Rather, we should realize that it is even more difficult for a Christian to fall. Even though some may say, "It is very easy for us to fall," we could not fall even if we wanted to without God allowing it. The only reason we can fall is that God is willing to allow us to fall into a trial that exposes our weaknesses.

A person who has not fallen once after his salvation does not have a strong experience of salvation and is not very deep in spiritual life. Such a person may not have fallen, but he is not truly standing either. At the most he is lying down. A person who is lying down can never fall. It is still possible to have an outward appearance of being an active Christian, because even people who are lying down can still roll around on the ground. Other Christians may not be lying down, but they are still merely sitting; consequently, it is not easy for them to fall either. The people who fall most easily are those who are not only standing but even more who are walking and running. Those who follow the Lord intensely will fall the most, and the more intensely a person runs, the more serious will be his falls.

Some may say that it is not a good thing to fall, but falling is very beneficial. Anyone who has not fallen is not deep in the Lord. Those who are deep in the Lord are those who have fallen and risen numerous times. Their spiritual life involves both days and nights, springs and autumns, summers and winters, and sunny days and cloudy days. In their living there are risings and fallings. As such, their living is in the hand of God, who has no intention for them to remain on a straight path.

Some may say that this is a dangerous way to speak. However, it is not dangerous in any way. Without the Lord's mercy, we could not rise up even if we wanted to, and without the Lord's willingness, we could not fall even if we wanted to. Those with sufficient experience will worship the Lord and bow down to Him, saying, "Lord, You have the authority over death and life. You have separated day from night. You have led me with Your light during the day, but You have also led me through darkness. Everything is of You. You have been present throughout the entire course of my life." Jacob, in his old age, had this view, and at the end of his days he worshipped God, leaning on the top of his staff and speaking of Him as "the God who has shepherded me all my life to this day" (Heb. 11:21; Gen. 48:15). Jacob's staff was not a proof of his shepherding of others but of Jacob's being shepherded by God. God's hand is supporting me; when I fall, I am still in His hand. He leads me in every circumstance, whether it is a rising or a falling. He is my Shepherd.

WORSHIPPING GOD AND ACKNOWLEDGING
THAT EVERYTHING IS OF GOD

If we have fallen, we should not be too sorrowful; rather, we should worship God. If we are able to stand, we should not be proud; rather, we should worship God. We should realize that the fall that one person experiences today may be our experience tomorrow (Gal. 6:1; 1 Cor. 10:12), and the stand that one person experiences today may be our experience tomorrow. We may be standing when another falls. However, it is quite possible that when he rises up, we may fall. God gives us a night when we ask Him for a day; He gives us a day when we are at ease with our night. God gives us situations that are contrary to our preferences in order to work Himself into us. Our thoughts are focused on a straight path, but His thoughts include ups and downs. Our expectations are based on the thought of a straight path, but God's principles, ways, and methods involve curves.

We are in God's hand; we did not determine the date of our birth or the time of our salvation. Consequently, we should not assume that the path ahead of us is in our hands. There is no need to be overly discouraged or sorrowful, much less boastful or proud, because everything is in His hand. He will have mercy on whomever He will have mercy, and He will have compassion on whomever He will have compassion (Rom. 9:15). He will visit whomever He will. He often comes to people in the dark of a "night," and He often meets people when their "sky" is cloudy and overcast. We touch Him more when we are suffering, and we grow more when we are in distress.

May the Lord have mercy on us so that we may increasingly worship Him, submit to Him, and trust in Him. May we not be proud but humble, bowing down to Him, worshipping Him, and praising Him. When we stand, may we acknowledge His grace, and when we fall, may we receive His dealing. May we see His considerations when our circumstances are smooth, and may we realize His special visitation when our circumstances are difficult. He wants to lead us to walk on a way that is more difficult but also deeper, a way that often is beyond our understanding. Nevertheless, we need not be fearful or anxious, and it is foolish to be boastful or proud. Those who have spiritual light will not be discouraged or proud, much less compare themselves with others, because they realize that everything is in God's hand. God gives life and allows death; He both exalts people and brings people low (Matt. 23:11; James 4:10; 1 Pet. 5:6); He causes people to ascend and to descend (Eph. 4:9); He leads people to a bright day and also leads them to a dark night; He provides smooth circumstances and adverse situations (Psa. 23:2, 4). This is a law in the universe and in spiritual matters.

Through these changing circumstances we grow by being broken and delivered from the self. When we are reduced, He is enlarged. When we decrease, He increases (John 3:30). Regardless of how much we change, the intention behind His hand never changes. No matter how He deals with us, either by touching or by seemingly not touching us, His hand upon us has a consistent purpose from beginning to end; that is, He wants to work in us to the extent that we will be filled with all that He is.

No matter whether we have fallen or have stood in the past, we should worship God. We need to prostrate ourselves before Him, confess that we are untrustworthy, and acknowledge that His grace is upon us. We need to ask God to open our eyes so that we may know His ways and so that our thoughts may be adjusted.

CHAPTER SIX

FAILURES ENABLING MAN
TO EXPERIENCE MORE OF GOD

Scripture Reading: Psa. 51:16-17; Luke 15:23-24; 2 Cor. 12:8-9

In the previous chapter we saw that God does not lead us on a straight path; it is a path that has ups and downs. In this chapter we will see that failures enable us to experience more of God.

FAILURES BEING PRECIOUS

As humans, we appreciate victory more than failure, and as children of God, we would be very satisfied if we experienced no failures in our daily living. From our experience, however, we should realize that failure is more precious than victory. When I say this, I have no intention of encouraging us to fail. It is useless to encourage someone to experience failure, and it is useless to encourage someone to seek victory. Whether a person stands or falls is unrelated to the encouragement he receives. We may think that we are able to stand because we are strong or that we will fail because we are weak, but those who have sufficient experience know that it is not up to us whether we stand or fall.

Romans 14:4 says, "Who are you who judge another's household servant? To his own master he stands or falls." This word shows that our standing and our falling depend on the Lord. We were created by the Lord. Our life and our breath do not depend upon ourselves but upon the Lord. Likewise, our ability to stand and overcome does not depend on ourselves but on the Lord. On the one hand, the Lord encourages us to stand and not to fall, to go forward and not to shrink back, to be victorious and not to be defeated. On the other hand, none of these matters—

standing or falling, going forward or shrinking back, and being victorious or defeated—depends on ourselves. All these matters are in the Lord's hand.

EXPERIENCING THE RICHES OF GOD

We all are familiar with the Lord's story in Luke 15 concerning a certain man having two sons (vv. 11-32). This story illustrates a great principle that is difficult for many people to understand when they first begin to follow the Lord. Only those who have followed the Lord for a considerable period of time understand the principle that God's riches can be experienced only by those who have been defeated. Those who have never been defeated cannot experience the riches of God. The older son in Luke 15 apparently had no experience of failure, but he also had no enjoyment of his father's riches. Instead, it was the younger son who enjoyed the father's riches (vv. 23-24).

It is very difficult for someone who has never experienced failure to be saved. A person with no experience of failure is hindered from receiving salvation, because in his own eyes, he is perfect, strong, and able to stand. I knew a person who was very highly regarded by others, but he was also boastful. On one hand, he seemingly had a humble disposition, but on the other hand, he was boastful of the fact that he had never been in trouble and had never failed. He often said that many believers in Jesus and even preachers were inferior to him, even though he was an unbeliever. From his perspective, he truly was an excellent man.

One day, when I was sitting with a senior co-worker, I asked, "How can we help such a person?" He said, "Brother, your friend is like the older son in Luke 15, who kept his father's orders and never disobeyed his father. Just like this older son, your friend has never fallen and has never been in trouble." Then the senior co-worker asked me, "Why do you think that your friend needs salvation?" I replied, "He needs salvation because he is still a sinner." The co-worker said, "Yes, he is a sinner in Adam, but he is not a sinner in his own eyes." Then I asked, "What should we do? How can he be saved?" The senior co-worker replied with a very interesting word. He said, "It is not enough for him to recognize that he is a sinner in Adam. In order for him to be saved, he must also see that he is a sinner in himself. He has to pass through a great fall and suffer a great defeat in order for him to be willing to be saved." I said, "But it is dangerous to experience such a great fall." He replied, "Are you more concerned for your friend than God is? Look at the younger son. God allowed him to fall so far that he eventually was in a distant place dwelling with hogs. God allowed him to be in such a situation because only those who fall can enjoy the riches of God. Your friend needs to fall; without falling, he cannot be saved." I said, "I do not like to hear that a person cannot be saved unless he falls." The co-worker said, "I understand, but it is not easy for an 'older' son to be saved. It is the 'younger' sons who are saved."

What does it mean to be an "older" son? Anyone who stands and does not fall is an "older" son. Upon hearing such a word, some will probably say, "Okay, let us all fall," but it is not up to us whether we stand or fall. Just as obeying God's commands is not up to us, being indifferent to God's commandments, like the younger son who fell to the point of living with hogs, is also not up to us.

The senior co-worker finally asked me, "Brother, do you know God's salvation or not?" I said, "Of course, I know. The Lord Jesus died for us by shedding His precious blood. When we believe in Him, we are saved. This is God's salvation." He said, "What you have said is just doctrine; it is useless. According to experience, the younger son knew salvation, and the older son did not. If you have never fallen or been defeated, you are an older son, and you do not know what salvation is." Then the co-worker asked me, "Have you ever fallen? Have you ever failed? Have you ever lived like a prodigal son?" I answered, "I have lived like a prodigal son more than the younger son in Luke 15." Then he said, "Praise the Lord, you know God's salvation."

RECEIVING GRACE THROUGH FAILURES

When a person who has followed the Lord for many years looks back and considers his past, he will worship the Lord and say, "Lord, all the failures that caused me grief have turned out to be blessings." When we fail, we touch and gain the Lord the most. Persons who have no "holes" cannot know God's grace; only those who have been broken can know God's grace.

Consider the story of King David. From his youth, whether in the eyes of his father, his brothers, or King Saul, David was pious and blameless. We all admire his condition. However, this pious person did not truly know God's grace or experience His riches; consequently, God loosened His grip on David. Once God loosened His grip, David's integrity fell apart, and his whole being was affected. When he fell, everyone who knew him probably felt that he was finished because of the seriousness of his failure. This was even David's feeling about himself. In Psalm 51 he said, "You do not delight in sacrifice; / Otherwise I would offer it; / You take no pleasure in burnt offerings. / The sacrifices of God are a broken spirit; / A broken and a contrite heart, O God, You will not despise" (vv. 16-17). David said that his spirit and heart were broken. A broken spirit is a sacrifice to God, and a broken heart will not be despised by God. David's spirit and heart were broken not because of misery or suffering but because of his failure, his fall. He hated his failure to such an extent that both his spirit and heart were broken. Despite his failure, God bestowed grace on him because he was a broken person. God can bestow His grace on a person who has a broken spirit and a broken heart.

Some saints have been saved for more than ten years, yet they remain intact, without any change in their being. They seemingly have never fallen or been in trouble; they are complete in themselves. However, such persons have little experience of grace or knowledge of God. Those who experience God's grace and know God are those who have experienced serious failures. Such failures break a person in his spirit and in his heart.

BEING BROKEN THROUGH FAILURES

There are many mysterious things in the universe. Although we prefer the light of the day, the darkness of the night is often more useful in God's hand. Although we long for situations full of peace, situations full of suffering are often more useful in God's hand. In the same principle, we long for victory, but we have little realization that our failures enable God to give us more grace. We desire to be strong, but we have little realization that our weaknesses enable us to profit from God's riches. God will never remove all our weaknesses; He will allow some weaknesses to remain with us throughout our human life. Those who have some spiritual experience know that when we are strong, it is not easy to experience the Lord. Rather, when we are weak, when we cannot rise up to speak for the Lord, to pray, or to bear responsibility, and when we have no strength to handle difficulties, we experience and enjoy the Lord.

Our weaknesses, however, are not as precious as our failures. Did David experience and know more of God before his fall or after his fall? Only after his fall did he know more of God, experience more of God, and gain more of God. Failures cause a person who is whole in himself to be broken. Once he is broken, he can receive the great benefit of God working Himself into him.

A brother who is seemingly perfect and who has never experienced any trouble has little room in his being to receive grace and to know God. Although there is no "hole" in his being, there also is no entrance in his being for God. Without a "hole," it is not easy for God's grace to enter into him. Such a brother can attend meetings in an ordinary way, sometimes sleeping during the meeting and sometimes saying Amen. He can meet week after week, month after month, and year after year, but neither can he go forward or backward.

Another brother may progress very well after his salvation, but then, inexplicably, he falls, backslides, and no longer meets for several years. However, just when we think that he has been lost completely, he will come back, and he will be different than he was before. He will bear the marks of being broken. When he speaks, he will speak with humility and tears concerning his failures, and even though he has been away for several years, his words will help and encourage us more than our words will help and encourage him. I am not suggesting that a brother should not meet for several years in order to be able to give an encouraging testimony of recovery. Rather, I am only pointing out that there will be some genuine breaking and genuine supply in those whom God has led through a period of failure.

Many years ago, there was a brother in northern China who passed through this kind of situation. He fell and could not rise up for several years. After he came back, he said, "Brother, it is hard for me to understand why I fell and could not rise up." I responded, saying, "It is not difficult to understand what happened. You were a self-righteous and self-justified person who needed to pass through a serious fall, a serious failure. Before your fall, you relied on yourself, boasted in yourself, and had full confidence in yourself. If God had not allowed you to have such a serious fall, how would you have ever known your true condition? You would have never lost confidence in yourself if you had simply not met for a few days. However, since you did not meet for three years, you know your real condition. In your present condition you are a broken person, and your spirit and heart have been broken as well."

Some people exhort others to be humble, but this is not helpful. We should be humble, but we should not exhort others to be humble, because such exhortations are futile. We need to realize that genuine humility comes from failures. A fallen and broken person spontaneously is a humble person. Some saints boastfully say, "I have never missed a meeting; I have never fallen." Nevertheless, in order for such a person to grow and advance, he needs some experience of failure. The way to receive grace involves failure, and failures come when God loosens the grip of His hand on us.

God is not concerned with our failures because He wants us to know ourselves and to have no confidence in ourselves; He wants our spirit and our heart to be broken. God treasures and desires a broken spirit and a broken heart because those who have a broken spirit and broken heart will be able to enjoy Him as grace. God's greatest desire is that we would experience and enjoy Him, fully tasting of all that He is and has. However, we are incapable of complying with God's desire. We think that we are able and sufficient; we rely on ourselves and have confidence in ourselves. Therefore, God is willing to loosen His grip and to allow us to fall and fail like a prodigal son.

MAN BEING ALLOWED TO FAIL

In Luke 15, the father, who represents God, acted differently than we would as parents. When the younger son said to his father, "Give me the share of the estate that falls to me," the father readily gave him his share (v. 12). The father did not respond by trying to exhort and persuade him to choose differently or by withholding his portion of the estate. Most parents would have responded in this way, but the father immediately gave the younger son his portion of the estate. Even when the son was leaving, the father did not try to restrain him. It seems as if the father was very hardhearted and did not love his son very much, because he simply gave up on him.

This is often how God treats us. He allows us to fail. He allows us to leave with what we have and lets us fall. However, when the younger son returned after wasting all his inheritance and living with hogs, the father blessed his son with his riches, and they all were merry and rejoicing. The father rejoiced because his son had died and was made alive again and had been lost and was found (vv. 24, 32). Anyone who has not died and who has never been lost is an "older son" who cannot fully enjoy his father's love and his father's riches.

I hope that we can see this deep principle: One who has never fallen or failed cannot know God, experience God, or enjoy God. God has no way to work Himself into a person who has no "holes." In order for God to enter into us for our experience and enjoyment, we must experience repeated failures.

MAN BEING BROKEN BY FAILURE
TO EXPERIENCE GOD

Blessed are those who fall; blessed are those who fail. Blessed are those who have not been meeting for a long while, blessed are those who cannot rise up, and blessed are those who are weak. Our inability to rise up, our falls, our failures, our forsaking of the meetings, and our backsliding only enable us to be broken. When our spirit and heart are broken and contrite, we will prostrate ourselves before God and say, "No one is more pitiful than I; no one is weaker than I; no one has failed more than I; no one is in a worse condition than I." When we can say these words, we will be blessed, and we will even hear God saying, "Bring out quickly the best robe and put it on him, and put a ring on his hand and sandals on his feet.

And bring the fattened calf; slaughter it, and let us eat and be merry, because this son of mine was dead and lives again; he was lost and has been found" (vv. 22-24).

The benefit of failure is that we are broken; the advantage of failure is that we enjoy God. We should not look down upon the failures in our Christian journey. Those who are experienced, who know God, and who are deep in the Lord will be able to say, "Thank You that You allowed me to fail so many times. Praise You that Your hand did not so quickly rescue me. Rather than praising You for rescuing me so quickly, I will praise You for not rescuing me quickly. I worship You that You have allowed me to fall and fail and even that You have allowed me to be indifferent and to backslide. I praise You that my many failures and my frequent backsliding have enabled me to know myself and to be broken before You. My heart is broken, and my spirit is broken. Although I cannot lift up my head before others, I have received Your grace and experienced You. Because of my weaknesses and failures, I can know You, experience You, and gain You." The more we follow Him, the more we will know the sweetness and preciousness of our failures. I am not encouraging us to fail; rather, I am thankful that our failures bring in the enjoyment of God as grace.

CHAPTER SEVEN

GOD'S GOAL BEING TO ENTER INTO MAN AND MINGLE HIMSELF WITH MAN

Scripture Reading: Exo. 33:14-16; John 5:19; 14:10

Some saints wonder why we experience God more through failure than through victory and why God's leading often involves experiences of failure. According to our concept, God's graciousness should lead us into victory. Consequently, when God allows us to fail, we assume that He is displeased with us. Our experience, however, reveals that this concept is not accurate. On the contrary, God allows us to fail because He wants to give us grace. In order to understand this matter clearly, we need to speak of God's goal.

GOD'S GOAL BEING TO ENTER INTO MAN AND MINGLE HIMSELF WITH MAN

God's goal for man is not related to avoiding failure or to achieving victory. God's unique goal for His chosen ones is to enter into them and to mingle Himself with them. In eternity past and in His creation of man, God's considerations were related to His intention to enter into man and to mingle Himself with man. This is a plain and simple statement, but it conveys the desire within God's heart. God's consideration of man's significance is related to His desire and ability to mingle Himself with man. Man's usefulness and function in relation to God are connected to his capacity to be mingled with God.

Man is mentioned first in the Bible in the context of God's intention related to His creation of man. At the time of man's creation, the Triune God held a council and decided to create man, saying, "Let Us make man in Our image, according to Our likeness" (Gen. 1:26). God created man in His image and according to His likeness in order to give man the capacity to be mingled with Him.

A Christian has a dual nature, including both divinity and humanity. A Christian has more than just the human nature; the Christian life is a hybrid life. Those who grow fruit trees know that the significance of grafting is the mingling of two lives to produce a hybrid nature. Christians have a hybrid nature, a dual nature, that is the product of the mingling of divinity with humanity. When we were unbelievers, God was God and man was man; we lived independently of the divine nature. However, in God's chosen ones, God and man and man and God have been mingled as one.

GOD DESIRING TO ENTER INTO MAN
TO BE GOD IN MAN,
AND ALSO DESIRING THAT MAN ENTER
INTO HIM TO BE MAN IN GOD

God did not want to be alone in the universe. Consequently, He created man to be a counterpart for Himself (cf. 2:18). God does not want to be God merely in Himself; He wants to enter into man to be God in man. He is God, but He desires to be mingled with man. In the same principle, God created man because He wants man to be mingled with Him. Although He wants man to be man, He wants man to be man in Him. Just as He does not want to be alone in the universe, He does not want man to be man merely in himself. He wants man to be man in God.

Although the thought of man being man in God may seem difficult to understand, it can be simply illustrated with sugar and water. In order to fully enjoy the taste of sugar, we often mix it with water. If we try to eat sugar by itself, it is dry and sticks to our mouth. However, when we mix sugar with water, it dissolves, and we can easily receive and enjoy it by drinking the sugar water. We are like a dry cube of sugar, but when we are put into God, the full flavor of man, who is in God's image and likeness, is manifested. Similarly, God is like the water. A glass of water can quench our thirst, but without sugar, its flavor is not fully realized. When God is put into man, the full flavor of God is expressed. God does not like to be alone; He wants to be mingled with man. Furthermore, God does not want man to be alone; He wants man to be mingled with Him.

Our concept of what God wants is limited primarily to matters related to good and ethical behavior; it does not occur to us that God wants us to be mingled with Him. Nevertheless, God's thoughts are higher than our thoughts (Isa. 55:9). God's goal for us is not confined to good and ethical behavior. He wants us to receive all that He is, and He further wants us to be mingled with Him. A moral person at the most is like a white sugar cube, clean and square. However, a moral person who is not in God will not be able to express the full flavor of God.

Every kind of food tastes better when it is seasoned. A person who is not in God is like unseasoned food. We may claim that we have been "seasoned," but our "seasonings" only include things related to wickedness, lust, and the world. None of these "seasonings" produce a sweet odor in our being. In God's salvation, however, the Lord's precious blood washes us of the things related to wickedness, lusts, and a love for the world and "seasons" us with the Holy Spirit. When the Holy Spirit, who is God Himself, is mingled with our spirit, we have a fresh and new "scent" in us. This is what God wants to do in us.

God has a desire to come into man to be God in man as well as a desire for man to enter into God to be man in God. I hope that we will see this matter and also learn to speak such a word. This is God's goal in the universe. It is not good for God to be alone. He desires to enter into man to be God in man; this occurred when the Lord Jesus was born in Bethlehem (Matt. 2:1). The thirty-three and a half years of the Lord Jesus' life as a Nazarene is a record of God entering into man to manifest Himself as God in man. God not only came from heaven to the earth, but He also entered into man to be God in man. All the life and living of the Lord Jesus on earth are a record of God being God in man.

Through the Lord's death and resurrection, the believers have been saved and regenerated and have been brought into God so that man could be man in God. God is in every Christian, but every Christian is also in God. The proper living of a Christian manifests the mingling of two natures, that is, the mingling of divinity in humanity and humanity in divinity.

When we see a believer with a proper living according to the mingling of God and man, we sense both a human flavor and a divine flavor. Although we sense that he is fully human, we also sense that he bears the flavor of God.

FAILURES ENABLING GOD TO BE MINGLED WITH MAN

God allows us to fail so that He can mingle Himself with us. People who seemingly never fail do not have much experience of mingling. It is as if they have only good humanity but with no divinity. When such a one stands, his standing comes out of himself without anything of God. He may not fail, but his victory comes only from his self-effort. Without some genuine failure, it is difficult for God to enter into him as grace and to be mingled with him. Without a crack in his being, nothing can enter into him, even God. Such a one is sufficient in himself and has no real understanding of what it means to rely on God. He is sufficient in himself to stand, to overcome, and to deal with every matter.

However, God is not looking for a person who is merely able to stand and overcome in himself. God wants a person into whom He can enter and with whom He can be mingled. It is truly regrettable that a person can seemingly be so strong that he can stand without God and so powerful that he can overcome without God. Although he may seem to stand and overcome, he does not have God. A person who only has good humanity is not what God desires. God wants to enter into man and mingle Himself with man so that man may manifest God's divinity in his humanity. Any person who thinks that he is sufficient in himself has no need for God.

When such a one comes to the meeting, he can even give glory to God, saying, "Hallelujah! Although I was tried, I stood firm; although I was tempted, I overcame." What he is really saying is that God can remain in heaven and that there is no need for God to enter into him, because he can glorify God and accomplish His will all by himself. Do you think that God would be satisfied with such a testimony? What do you think God would say to such a believer? I believe that God would be displeased and would say, "You are satisfied, but I am not. You may seem to be standing without any failure and seem to be victorious without any defeat, but you will certainly fail." If a believer can bear the weight of a certain amount of pressure, God will double the amount. If a doubling of the amount is not enough, He will allow the pressure to increase even more. God is able to break even the strongest believer. A believer who is able to stand when a certain amount of pressure comes should not be confident that he will be able to stand indefinitely. Eventually, a believer who has confidence in himself will have a great fall, a serious fall. He will fall to the extent that his actions will be beyond comprehension and even be manifested before all the saints in the church.

If a person falls to such an extent, it is only because he is so strong in himself and even says to himself, "I can stand firm, and I can overcome. I am sufficient in myself." We need to remember that God hates our "I" the most, and He will use any means in order to allow our "I" to be exposed and to fall. There are many means that God can use to expose our self. He can use everything in the universe to assist Him in accomplishing His goal. He can use our family circumstances, including children and even grandchildren. He will give us the circumstances that we need in order to expose us. When God allows it, a man can fall to the uttermost. When a person falls in this way, he is more easily broken because he begins to understand what it really means to rely on God, to experience God, and to have God mingled with him. We need to see that God's desire for us is not related to either our victory or defeat. God's attention is not focused on victory or defeat, standing or falling; God's only desire is to have an opportunity to enter into us and to be mingled with us.

BEING FEARFUL OF GOD'S ABSENCE
MORE THAN BEING FEARFUL OF FAILURE

In my youth, someone who loved the Lord very much impressed me deeply with the matter of pride. At that time I saw that when we are proud, we will fall (Prov. 16:18; 1 Tim. 3:6). I also saw the need to be in fear and trembling lest we fall. This principle has helped me continually for decades. However, in recent years and through God's mercy, I have learned that it is not enough to merely be fearful of falling. There is something far more serious than falling—God's absence. In whatever we do, we should be more fearful of God being absent in our actions than we are of merely falling or making a mistake. We need to consider whether God is absent in what we are doing. It is not enough for me to give a message; God must be in my giving of the message. If God is not in it, it will be a terrible thing. We should be fearful of God's absence. These three words—*God is absent*—are quite sobering.

Moses knew God in the Old Testament age. Moses was eighty years old when he was called by God, and he suffered many trials and dealings throughout his life. In Psalm 90:10, he said, "The days of our years are seventy years, / Or, if because of strength, eighty years." According to Moses' estimation, a person who reaches eighty years of age is past the normal age of death. Because of God's selection and calling, however, Moses was used by God to lead the children of Israel, even when he was past the normal age of death.

When Moses was called, God showed him a vision: "The Angel of Jehovah appeared to him in a flame of fire out of the midst of a thornbush. And when he looked, there was the thornbush, burning with fire; but the thornbush was not consumed" (Exo. 3:2; Acts 7:30). Through the thornbush and the fire, God showed Moses a type of mingling, and Moses realized that everything was of God and that nothing was of himself. It was as if God spoke to Moses, saying, "You are a thornbush. I am Jehovah, and as the flame of fire, I will burn you, but you will not be consumed. My glory and My power will be manifested through you. I will use your person, but I will not use your strength as the fuel of My fire. I will use you to lead the children of Israel out of Egypt and will deal with Pharaoh through you, but I will not use your strength. You are the thornbush, and I am the fire in the thornbush. I want you to cooperate with Me and be a vessel for Me to display My strength." When God called Moses in this way, He showed Moses the matter of God being mingled with man.

The children of Israel, however, did not see this matter. When they rejected God by worshipping an idol at the foot of Mount Sinai, God came to Moses and said, "Go, get down; for your people, whom you brought up out of the land of Egypt, have corrupted themselves" (Exo. 32:7), and then He said, "Now go, lead the people to the place about which I have spoken to you" (v. 34). Moses, however, responded by saying, "Consider also that this nation is Your people" (33:13). This response indicates that Moses realized the children of Israel had been rescued through Jehovah's strength, not his strength. Thus, they were God's people.

Then Moses prayed, saying, "If Your presence does not go with us, do not bring us up from here. For how then shall it be known that I have found favor in Your sight, I and Your people? Is it not by Your going with us, so that we, I and Your people, are distinct from all the other people who are on the face of the earth?" (vv. 15-16). This indicates that Moses knew he could not bear this responsibility in himself and even that he would not bear the responsibility in himself. This is a prayer of one who knows God. How many times have the elders in the churches prayed such a prayer, saying, "God, if You do not bear the responsibility with us, we will quit"? This is my secret before God. I often pray, "O Lord, if You are not working in me, if You do not bear the responsibility with me, I will quit. I will resign and go fishing; I will go to Egypt and take the way of the world. This is Your responsibility, not mine. I am just like Moses, who was only a shepherd, and like Peter, who was only a fisherman. Nevertheless, You called me, telling me that You would work through me. Now, if You want me to do everything by myself, I will quit." This prayer does not sound respectful, but the Holy Spirit can testify that I often pray in this way. I have said to the Lord, "If You do not come, I will not do anything. If You do not go, I will not go. I have to give a message today, but if You are not in it, I will not speak. Whether I speak or do not speak is not up to me; it is up to You. The church belongs to You. The saints belong to You. They are Your people. If they are hungry, You must feed them. You are their Father; I am only a laborer. Whether or not Your children are fed is Your responsibility. So if You are not in my speaking, I will not speak."

Rather than begging God, as we usually do, we should be like Moses, who was adamant in his speaking to God. It was as if he pointedly asked, "God, are You going or not?" and then said, "If You are going, I will work; if You do not go, I can only resign. It is Your decision whether or not to go; it is not mine." Like Moses, we must live according to the principle of being a person with two natures that have been mingled together. In everything we do, we need to check to see if God is in it, even in such matters as visiting a friend or speaking a simple word to someone else. We need to ask, "Is God in it?"

It is not enough to be fearful of making mistakes or of falling. We also need to be afraid of God being absent in our actions. We need to ask whether or not God is present in our actions and in our goings forth. Even when the Lord Jesus was on the earth, He said, "The words that I say to you I do not speak from Myself, but the Father who abides in Me does His works" (John 14:10). Although the Lord was speaking, it was the Father who was doing His works. This should also be our experience when we speak. Although we are speaking, it must be God who is doing His work. He should be mingled with us and working in our speaking. Then our speaking will be His speaking because He and we are mingled as one. Although we are speaking, it will really be God who is speaking in us. Although He is God, He does not speak directly from heaven; instead, He enters into man and speaks through man. This is the experience of a Christian who lives according to his mingled natures.

This is also the way that should be manifested in every aspect of our Christian life, including our daily living. Daily and hourly, when we do something, whether great or small, we should be able to say, "I am not here alone, God is here. I am not doing something out from myself, but God is doing it in me and with me."

GOD'S DESIRE BEING TO ENTER
INTO MAN TO BE GOD IN MAN

When we truly learn this lesson, we will be able to avoid many failures because in our experiences of being broken, we will learn to know ourselves, deny ourselves, have no confidence in ourselves, and not depend on ourselves. As we are about to do something, we will be focused more on not losing God's presence and on God working in us than we will be of failures. Whenever we do anything, we should be prostrate before God and say, "O Lord, if You do not go, I will not move; if You are absent, I will not do anything. This whole matter depends on You, not on me. I am afraid that You may not be in this matter. I am afraid that I may do something in myself. I am afraid of standing and even of being victorious in myself. God, I am even more afraid of being successful in myself than of failing, and I am more afraid of standing by myself than of falling. I would rather fall than stand alone; I would rather fail than be successful alone. I am fearful of standing and of being successful without You. I want to learn to do only those things that come out of my being mingled with You. I only want to live and to work in a mingled way."

God allows us to fail when we neglect this lesson and do not learn it. Our concept is much lower than God's concept. We think that God's goal for us is to overcome, to stand, and to be victorious. However, this is not God's concept. His goal is not for us to overcome, to stand, or to be successful but for Him to enter into us and to be mingled with us.

God desires to enter into man to be God in man; He also wants man to enter into God to be man in God. We need to ask ourselves whether this is our Christian life. In our living, do we allow God to come into us to be God in man, and do we enter into God to be man in God? If we have such a life, we do not have to be concerned with defeat or victory. We should focus on this glorious fact: God has entered into us to be God in man, and we have entered into God to be man in God. If we do not see this glorious fact, we will fail and fall. If we do not see this glorious fact, any "standing" that we exhibit will be worthless because it will not be according to the mingled living of a proper Christian. We should praise the Lord that when we stand and overcome in ourselves, God allows us to fail and fall. When everything is seemingly smooth, God allows us to fail and fall in order to break and expose us to the point that we will say, "Lord, I know that Your goal is to enter into me to be God in me and for me to enter into You to be man in You. Thank You that Your desire is to be practically mingled with me." God's being mingled with us, rather than our standing, overcoming, failing, or falling, is all that matters.

ABOUT THE AUTHOR

Witness Lee was born in 1905 in northern China and raised in a Christian family. At age 19 he was fully captured for Christ and immediately consecrated himself to preach the gospel for the rest of his life. Early in his service, he met Watchman Nee, a renowned preacher, teacher, and writer. Witness Lee labored together with Watchman Nee under his direction. In 1934 Watchman Nee entrusted Witness Lee with the responsibility for his publication operation, called the Shanghai Gospel Bookroom.

Prior to the Communist takeover in 1949, Witness Lee was sent by Watchman Nee and his other co-workers to Taiwan to ensure that the things delivered to them by the Lord would not be lost. Watchman Nee instructed Witness Lee to continue the former's publishing operation abroad as the Taiwan Gospel Bookroom, which has been publicly recognized as the publisher of Watchman Nee's works outside China. Witness Lee's work in Taiwan manifested the Lord's abundant blessing. From a mere 350 believers, newly fled from the mainland, the churches in Taiwan grew to 20,000 in five years.

In 1962 Witness Lee felt led of the Lord to come to the United States, settling in California. During his 35 years of service in the U.S., he ministered in weekly meetings and weekend conferences, delivering several thousand spoken messages. Much of his speaking has since been published as over 400 titles. Many of these have been translated into over fourteen languages. He gave his last public conference in February 1997 at the age of 91.

He leaves behind a prolific presentation of the truth in the Bible. His major work, *Life-study of the Bible,* comprises over 25,000 pages of commentary on every book of the Bible from the perspective of the believers' enjoyment and experience of God's divine life in Christ through the Holy Spirit. Witness Lee was the chief editor of a new translation of the New Testament into Chinese called the Recovery Version and directed the translation of the same into English. The Recovery Version also appears in a number of other languages. He provided an extensive body of footnotes, outlines, and spiritual cross references. A radio broadcast of his messages can be heard on Christian radio stations in the United States. In 1965 Witness Lee founded Living Stream Ministry, a non-profit corporation, located in Anaheim, California, which officially presents his and Watchman Nee's ministry.

Witness Lee's ministry emphasizes the experience of Christ as life and the practical oneness of the believers as the Body of Christ. Stressing the importance of attending to both these matters, he led the churches under his care to grow in Christian life and function. He was unbending in his conviction that God's goal is not narrow sectarianism but the Body of Christ. In time, believers began to meet simply as the church in their localities in response to this conviction. In recent years a number of new churches have been raised up in Russia and in many eastern European countries.